BELONGING
TO
CHRIST

BELONGING
TO
CHRIST

Catholic Poetry

Christina M. Sorrentino

Art Work
All images are in the public domain or are licensed under the
Unsplash/Pixabay License as royalty free photos.

Cover Image: Juan de Juanes, Wikimedia Commons
Pg. 16: Josh Applegate, Unsplash
Pg. 19: Shalone Cason, Unsplash
Pg. 22: Josh Applegate, Unsplash
Pg. 25: Mateus Campos Felipe, Unsplash
Pg. 27: Florentino V. Floro, Wikimedia Commons
Pg. 30: Jacob Bentzinger, Unsplash
Pg. 33: Mateus Campos Felipe, Unsplash
Pg. 35: Gabriella Clare Marino, Unsplash
Pg. 37: Christina M. Sorrentino
Pg. 39: Alex Braga, Unsplash
Pg. 41: Jackson David, Unsplash
Pg. 43: Aaron Burden, Unsplash
Pg. 45: John Wilson, Unsplash
Pg. 48: Christoph Schmid, Unsplash
Pg. 50: Marcaroni, Pixabay
Pg. 52: Jean-Baptiste Marie Pierre, Wikimedia Commons
Pg. 54: Giuseppe Bartolomeo Chiari, Wikimedia Commons
Pg. 56: Ludovico Carracci, Wikimedia Commons
Pg. 59: Filippo Lauri, Wikimedia Commons
Pg. 61: Grant Whitty, Unsplash
Pg. 64: Robert Nyman
Pg. 66: Florentino V. Floro: Wikimedia Commons
Pg. 69: El Greco: Wikimedia Commons
Pg. 71: Alex Perez, Unsplash
Pg. 73: Jean Auguste Dominique Ingres, Wikimedia Commons
Pg. 75: Juan Bautista Mayno, Wikimedia Commons
Pg. 78: Bartolomé Esteban Murillo, Wikimedia Commons
Pg. 80: Patrick Wittke, Unsplash

First Printing

This book is dedicated to all of our faithful Catholic
priests for their loving service to Christ and His Holy
Church, and for carrying out His mission of preaching,
serving, and sanctifying.

And especially to the priests of my parish,

Rev. Robert W. Dillon

Rev. Evangelio R. Suaybaguio

Rev. Neil A. Kelly

Rev. John Edison

Thank you for answering the call with fidelity, dedication,
and the self-giving that is the hallmark of the priesthood. We
need more good and holy priests like you, especially now,
more than ever.

Contents

Introduction

"There is nothing so great as the Eucharist. If God had something more precious, He would have given it to us."
Saint John Vianney

How can I have an intimate relationship with Christ that allows me to truly understand the plans He has for me? How will I be able to know, love, and serve Him in this world and be happy with Him; united with His Father and the Holy Spirit, forever in Heaven? What can I do to be able to listen to the voice of the Lord?

Embracing Christ

The Son of God is my Savior. He is my true Beloved, the One who gave up His life for me by suffering on the Cross so that I can spend eternity with the Triune God in paradise. As the Son having two natures; He is both true God and true man. And He is always present to me in my life as a millennial Catholic woman. I experience His love, consolation, and compassion by choosing to spend time in His Divine embrace. I remain with Him in the peace and serenity gifted to me by His Holy Presence.

The Eucharist, the Body Blood, Soul and Divinity of Christ, His crucified, resurrected, and glorified Body, becomes my refuge of safety. In the silence, I can share my concerns, frustrations, sadness, pain, joy, and happiness with Jesus. In return, He wraps me in His love. He helps me to strengthen my relationship with Him as I embrace the sacredness of these precious moments. This is His holy kiss from heaven on earth. I am His and He is mine.

We are called to have a Divine Romance with our beloved Spouse, to become ignited with the desire to completely empty our heart of self, and to fill it whole and entirely with God alone. We are all called to a life of holiness; to be united in heart, mind, and soul, with the Bridegroom who waits for His bride as she prepares herself to become spotless and without blemish.

Our vocation to love means that we surrender more and more of ourselves each day by letting go of the things that prevent us from becoming closer to the Lord. We should not focus solely on the vices that create a barrier between us and Christ, but rather keep our eyes fixed in a heavenly gaze on the virtues that we hope to attain as to one day be able to see the Lord Face to face. It is by partaking in the Paschal Banquet, and receiving the Body and Blood of Christ during the Holy Sacrifice of the Mass that we grow in holiness and intimacy with our Lord.

My Life Belongs to Christ

I know I cannot live without Jesus, nor would I ever have the desire to live without Him. I would be nothing without Him. Life without Christ at the center would mean going through the motions without any purpose or reason. When there is happiness and joy, who would I be able to thank? During the times I am confronted with challenges and difficulties, when I fall, who will be there to catch me? When I am sad and in a state of grief, who will be there to console me?

He is why I live my life. Jesus is always the Light in any darkness. And it is in the Catholic Church with the Blessed Sacrament that Jesus is always present to me and to all of us. It is in the tabernacle in every single Catholic Church around the world that He waits for us to visit Him. His Love for us radiates from His Most Sacred Heart. It is up to us to accept His Love and to love Him in return. The sanctuary lamp burns brightly, reminding us that Jesus is always present to us.

The collection of poetry in this book I hope can inspire you to share in the desire to want to have a deeper and more meaningful relationship with Christ. If you have been away from the Church, please, know that Jesus loves you and is waiting for you.

There is nothing you have done that cannot be forgiven by Christ, and He is longing for the day to offer you pardon for your sins in the beautiful sacrament of Confession. He wants to forgive you, if you let Him. The Son of God wants you to receive Him in the Eucharist; His most intimate expression of Love that He gives us on this earth; the gift of Himself.

--- Christina M. Sorrentino

BELONGING
TO
CHRIST

The Loud Silence

O glorious St. Joseph,
he is most chaste and just.
The Son of David
awakes from slumber;
takes the New Eve as his spouse.

Guardian of the Virgin,
who carries Jesus in her womb,
he protects God's Living Tabernacle;
the Ark of the Covenant, revealed.

In the shadows,
a hidden presence,
he plays a pivotal role.
In the story of salvation,
the Husband of Mary,
never utters a single word.

Faithful Foster-Father,
the Guardian of our Lord,
is entrusted with a precious treasure,
Jesus, the Divine Messiah,
Who becomes the cornerstone.

With the melody of self-surrender,
silence in a tumultuous world,
the obedient servant
quiets his own voice to listen;
follows the promptings of the Lord.

Love Divine

O beautiful Sacrament
he receives on bended knee,
with the imposition of hands,
the Holy Spirit besought from heaven,
stirs up the grace of God in him.

No longer one of many,
set apart from the crowd,
he is made sublime and venerable,
by the power of the Word.

With the Sacrament of Order,
imprints an indelible mark.
Consecrated to God alone
he dispenses the saving treasures of Christ,
with a pure and gentle heart.

By the power of his consecration,
the gift bestowed upon him,
in persona Christi Capitis,
he proclaims the Mystery.

Gifts of the Creator,
the work of human hands,
with the Dia-Logos,
transform upon the altar;
humanity drawn into Divinity.

Enkindled in the Divine fire,
their hearts beat as one,
the rhapsody of Trinitarian Love.

Sacramentum caritatis,
Paschal banquet,
wedding feast,
Christ unites Himself to His beloved bride,
with a kiss from heaven,
the consummation of Love Divine.

Beloved Priest

As the dawn slowly rises
until the heavy dark descends,
he marks the hours with the prayer,
that sanctifies the day.

With a zealous heart,
on fire with the word,
he breaks open the truth,
to those who thirst.

He acts as the Bridegroom,
at the supper of the Lamb.
Before the altar he stands,
in the person of Christ the Head.

Transubstantiation,
the sweet taste of heaven on earth,
the Kingdom is before us,
a precious gift of priceless worth.

With the outpouring of the Spirit,
his hands absolve us from our sins.
We receive pardon,
and the Body is made whole again.

As Christ the Physician,
the power of grace manifests.
By the sacred anointing the sick receive,
peace, courage, healing, and strength.

God's beloved priest,
is of immeasurable value.
For without his vocation,
we have nothing.

Holy Orders (Priesthood)

A brilliant, radiant essence,
embraces the sacred space,
with a Trinitarian echo,
the invitation to transcendence.

As the traditional chant,
Litaniæ sanctorum is sung,
a beautiful rhythm flows gracefully,
from cantor to congregants.

The candidate lay prostrate,
with the death of self,
as the praying Church calls upon,
the Communion of Saints.

An overwhelming Presence,
permeates the jubilant air,
as the Holy Spirit pours forth,
with the imposition of hands.

At the pivotal time,
the sacramental moment,
with the consecratory prayer,
constitutes the visible sign;
imparts an indelible character.

An overwhelming sense of pure elation,
the expression of exultant joy,
bursts forth about the Cathedral;
an indescribable experience of the soul.

After they are vested,
in the liturgical garb,
His priest sons are anointed,
with the Sacred Chrism,
consecrated for the service of God.

The peace and delight so sought,
a bliss until now unknown,
found in Christ Jesus,
through them love lays hold.

The faithful are endowed,
with an incredulous blessing;
the gift of the sacerdotal priesthood;
he becomes an alter Christus.

The Curé of Ars

St. John Vianney,
the Curé of Ars,
burning for love alone,
with his heart inflamed,
had only a desire for God.

The grace of suffering,
a gift from the Holy One,
he delighted in his heavy cross,
the sweet consolation from above.

As a humble parish priest,
he spent many hours a day,
as the minister of Penance,
in persona Christi.

Snatching souls,
from the clutches of the fiend,
he roused the fury of hell,
"the villainous."

The Curé's confessional,
the true miracle of Ars,
lead countless souls to sanctity,
saved from the wretched one.

Breathing the last breath,
he came to his final end;
Face to face with his Beloved,
a peaceful bliss,
eternal life with Him.

Forever Thine

Word made Flesh,
veiled before my eyes,
in a tiny white host,
the Hidden Christ is alive.

Gifts of His creation,
simple bread and wine,
humble offerings to the Father,
with the Breath of the Spirit
transform upon the altar;
the memorial of Christ's sacrifice.

Spotless Victim,
unblemished Lamb,
really and mysteriously made present,
the Lord's Body and Blood,
behold in the priest's hands.

Sacred banquet,
Paschal feast,
come to the Table,
receive the Holy Eucharist.

Called to communion,
heaven weds the earth;
a Divine invitation,
the Sacrament of Love.

Bread of Life,
Beloved of my heart,
overcome with joy,
I could die.
I am forever Thine.

O Bread of the Angels

An unbreakable bond,
of love forever intertwined,
unites Christ with His Body;
the spotless and unblemished bride.

He is the beloved Bridegroom
to the spouse of Christ, the Church.
Our eyes gaze upon Him,
as we adore the Hidden Lord,
veiled behind the consecrated host.

Jesus, we revere Him,
with eyes fixed upon
His Eucharistic Face;
our hearts a-burning,
by the stirring of grace.

With our Mother Mary,
we proclaim His Holy Name;
offering our humble fiat,
as we delight in Him.

Glorious Saint Joseph,
our patron and our guide,
leads us to the Sacred Heart of Jesus;
the center of our lives.

Jesus how we cherish,
the precious moments before Him;
the Real Presence,
the Most Holy Eucharist.

O Bread of the Angels,
sweet Sacrament of Love,
we seek Him in the silence,
when Heart speaks to heart.

In His Presence

The golden rays reflect,
through the little round glass.
In the center of the sunburst,
displays the Most Blessed Sacrament.

The stained-glass windows,
reflect a radiant glow.
His beauty and magnificence,
permeates the hallowed realm.

The bright grains of incense,
upon the red-hot charcoal,
the censer, thrice-swung
with fragrant smoke,
rises to the heavenly host.

From the sacred shadows,
adoring on his knees,
in the reverent stillness,
he worships Christ the Victim;
Christ the Priest.

Sun-kissed from His Love,
a burning flame within,
the light radiates outward,
and shines in perfect brilliance.

In This Sacrament

Drowning in sorrow,
swept away by the tide of sin,
the unclean oblation,
is the greatest evil within.

With grief of the soul,
and detestation,
a contrite heart renders,
towards reconciliation.

In perfect love
or with a torrent of fear,
hope for pardon springs forth,
with the infusion of grace
and a disposition sincere.

With the words of absolution,
by the power of the keys,
the Holy Breath of God,
looses the chains that bind,
and sets the prisoner free.

The Cup of Mercy,
with sanctification outpoured,
mends the broken Body;
for in this Sacrament,
union with God is restored.

Waking Dawn

A new beginning,
with hearts set on fire,
burn with a deep faith,
the most wondrous desire.

With a twirl of leaves,
and a whisper of the wind,
there is a most steadfast love;
the fiery flame found within.

There is a crown of autumn,
the sparkle of frost,
with a change of the tide,
some become lost.

The most beautiful joy,
an embrace by the Father,
He is a most loyal friend,
yet many turn to another.

A waking of dawn,
the toll of the bell,
when an echo is heard,
the rest bid farewell.

With a conversion of heart,
the wind can change course,
there is always hope;
a sense of remorse.

There is a deep sea of blue,
with no twinkle in the sky,
but the stars may return,
with the death of pride.

Hushed Truth

A shadow of silence
overcasts the woeful plea,
with the melancholic echo,
the faint whisper within me.

Upon the lofty mountain
where the snapdragons grow,
the sheep graze in the bright moonlight,
as the silhouette of a wolf howling
can be seen in the hemlock grove.

Lovely cascades gently fall,
down a simple black veil;
the shawl of illusion
obscures the darkness,
the most wicked nightmare.

A mist hovers low
o'er the wooded landscape,
as the splendor of the Sun
reveals the hushed truth,
that He will never forsake me.

In Bleak September

Ode to September,
to the bleakest of days,
when the bright summer has past;
autumn clasps the Cypress trees.

With the fluttering petals
of the dark crimson rose,
a choir sings the eulogic hymn;
the melody of the blackbird.

The tune of lament,
whispers in the breeze,
but the words of the psalms,
offer consolation and peace.

When everything turns upside down,
the world becomes upright.
For in His Kingdom suffering leads to glory;
the gift of eternal life.

Fountain of Grace

There is a pulsing crimson within my chest;
a mind grief-stricken full of deep distress.
Woe to the pining sadness and sorrow,
as the ruby red poppies bloom
to mark an eternal slumber.

With a burning desire to turn back the clock,
and breathe the unspoken words,
which never did depart,
I mourn the bleak, September silence.

As the tears of autumn
fall gently upon the rocky ground,
the roar of thunder echoes
through the ashen-colored clouds.

There is a montage of thoughts;
an intertwined thread,
the black and white memories
which I long to forget.

Ode to the quiet somber
with the soft pitter-patter of rain,
until the blue-violet emerges,
with the flow of healing waters
from the Fountain of Grace.

Follow Him

The devil's snare invades
the refuge of the sacred space;
once a dwelling of peace.

The serpent slithers at the side,
touches face-to-face
the putrid soul,
with a disposition of pride.

In the eerie stillness
with minutes until noon,
the lies from the evil one
convolutes the truth.

Masquerading as an angel of light,
with a hardened heart so cold,
the cruel breath of injustice
utters wicked words.

The cloud of unknowing,
drifts across the autumn sky,
as outside glitters like gold,
the darkness creeps inside.

A cracked windowpane,
shatters with broken glass.
The contraceptive mentality,
leads to an untimely death.

Across the Sea of Galilee,
the Bridegroom awaits
with love profound.
His voice still echoes loudly,
amidst the crowd.

A new journey,
begins with the first step,
as I pick up my cross once more,
and continue to follow Him.

Maranatha!

Virgin Mary,
Mother of God,
we wait with thee in joyful expectation,
for the birth of thy Incarnate Son.

God-bearer,
help us to prepare,
to make the way for our Savior,
Who heralds our salvation.

Hail Mary,
Tabernacle of God,
let us follow thee,
and discern His word.

Fair Maiden Mother,
the blossom of Nazareth,
teach us to ponder His ways,
in the depths of our heart.

Immaculate Mary,
Full of Grace,
in Advent we anticipate,
O Lord, come, maranatha!

Waiting on the Word

In the fullness of time,
it was long foretold,
by the holy prophets of Israel.

Behold the King,
sent forth from His throne,
Jesus, Mighty God.

Christ is the Logos,
the Eternal Word;
Incarnate utterance of God.

In the days of Herod,
came forth the Living Bread,
within the town of Bethlehem.

Born of the Virgin,
He is the Fruit of her womb,
called the Theanthropos; the God-man.

And lo, the angels spoke,
of Love's ultimate offering;
the chains and shackles of sin to be broken.

He lay in the manger
swaddled like a lamb.
He is the Savior, Redeemer of the world.

The Samaritan Woman

A yearning desire,
ignited a burning flame;
a fiery inferno,
one that could not be tamed.

Love beckoned her,
the truth beneath her bones,
hidden by the dusty surface;
deep within her soul.

It was a Divine invitation,
at the hour of midday.
There He did thirst,
with spoken words; her soul engraved.

The well water flowed,
reflecting the radiance of the Sun.
With a kiss from heaven,
she went forth to spread the word.

The Transfiguration

Upon the mountain,
beneath a canopy of powder blue,
with the veil removed,
the Face of Love showed,
the hidden glory of God revealed.

A luminous cloud ascended,
with the sound of His voice;
'twas upon Mt. Tabor,
the 'Wonder of Wonders,'
was radiant and dazzling white.

There was a moment of joy,
the foretaste of eternal bliss,
when a vision unfolded,
amidst the splendor of holiness.

Fallen to the ground,
eyes downcast in shame,
with a terrified glance,
the disciples felt unworthy,
to bask in His rays.

With a tender touch,
Christ's hand reached forth.
With uplifted chin,
the apostles beheld,
the Lover's gaze.

A crown beyond the cross,
beyond humiliation and pain,
His ultimate Triumph was,
the victory of Resurrection.

This Same Cup

Why must I drink once more
from the same cup;
the one of gall and vinegar,
sour grapes from the vine?

As tears trickle down,
I remember the bitter taste,
like an unripened apple,
picked too soon from the branch.

The offering of sweet drink,
I knew would not last.
A kind and gentle peace,
with a mother's healing touch,
shatters like a broken glass.

I beg the Lord for mercy,
cry aloud with a sorrowful plea.
With woeful words I beseech Him,
"Take this same cup from me."

Christ holds my hand
in the Garden of Gethsemane;
as He gazes into my eyes,
I desire to suffer with Thee.

I walk the road to Calvary,
stained with tears of blood.
My heart weeps profoundly,
as I am united with the begotten Son.

At the foot of the Cross,
I behold the spotless Lamb,
His blood poured upon the earth.
O the suffering of my Beloved,
not even the Son of God was spared.

Triumph of the Cross

O Christ Jesus,
the sacrificial Lamb,
hangs upon the wooden cross,
as the woeful women weep,
and the veil of darkness covers the land.

The wicked waters roar,
as the treacherous waves,
crash onto the shore.
With the slithering serpent,
hissing in the wind,
the swirling tempest,
rages in the sea.

At the Hour of Great Mercy,
the earth trembles,
as the light shatters through.
O blood and water
from His Sacred Heart gushes forth;
radiates the Truth.

A great paradox,
the Cross of Christ,
an instrument of suffering
becomes a symbol of faith;
death unto eternal life.

Hold Fast

At the midnight hour,
before the dawn
of the most somber day,
once the last echo of the "Gloria" chant
has faded into the night,
and the final toll of the bell,
is but a distant memory.

Darkness envelops the starless sky,
with the sound of the mourning dove.
The time has come,
to take the begotten Son.

Tears trickle down,
a rose-colored cheek,
with quivering lips
and glistening eyes;
before the pregnant pause,
comes forth a woeful sigh.

O sweet, sweet sorrow.
O happy lament.
A heart weeps profoundly,
as the Beloved is removed
from the Holy Tent.

As the Bridegroom departs,
a cold, chill permeates the air.
Amidst the silent, stillness
the most solemn day enters in.

With the dying embers
of the sanctuary flame,
the Repository is dismantled
as the last candle burns away.

As the rain drizzles down,
upon the chapel windowpane,
hope appears crucified,
but all is not as it seems.

The light from the waning moon,
shines through the stained-colored glass,
as the dogwood gently sways in the wind,
and creates a beautiful dance.

Within the depth of the soul,
lies a truth beneath our bones,
where expectant joy abides,
in the silence of the night.

For at the Vigil of Resurrection
with Pascal flame anew,
the "Lumen Christi" is sung;
after three days of bitter grief,
we celebrate the covenant fulfilled.

Death has no dominion,
swallowed up in victory,
the Lord is truly Risen.
Christ is alive indeed!

Paschal Candle

Easter candle
white as snow
made from beeswax
purity of Christ

the wick
Christ's humanity
the flame
His Divine Nature

bears the five wounds
the Lord's Passion
alpha and omega
beginning and the end

lit from the Great Fire
Vigil of Resurrection
the Risen Christ
Light of the World

flame flickers
dances to and fro
aglows ever brightly
dispels darkness

three times raised
Lumen Christi
comes into the world
rising in glory

most holy night
solemn of days
eternal presence
Love infinite

When Love Calls

A soft-spoken whisper,
o'er the tumultuous waves
of the restless sea,
as the days become longer,
His voice louder soundeth,
as He beckons,
"Come, follow me."

There before Him,
upon the waters of Galilee,
the brothers James and John
abandon their fishing nets,
leaving the drudge and toil,
they bid farewell,
to their father Zebedee.

A Divine invitation,
Jesus calls our name;
leads us to a quiet place
where we meet Him
behind the curtain,
and enter the inner sanctuary.

The lovely almond tree,
embower'd in its own green leaves,
bends and sways so gently,
as the honey bees hum softly.

O Christians come,
let us leave the vainglory behind;
to cast away the golden calf,
and let down our bitter pride.

Lo! A happy death,
the gift of Divine obedience,
put our own self to slumber,
and gaze upon the God of Wonders.

Let us take up our cross,
with Christ our source of strength,
journey with Him to Calvary,
as we begin now
our apprenticeship in holiness.

Lukewarm

O gracious Lord,
merciful Father,
rebukes the self-sufficient,
those who bring dishonor.

The spiritually complacent,
avert their wretched eyes,
with a spirit of indifference,
turn away from the Divine fire.

Half-hearted men,
fall away from Him,
with the dying of conviction;
the disease of unfaithfulness.

The beauty of water,
hot, cleanses and purifies,
cold, refreshes and enlivens,
but the lukewarm sicken Him;
are good for nothing.

O Christ Jesus,
He grants the gift of repentance;
a heart consumed by fervor,
becomes a true witness.

Our Lady of the Most Blessed Sacrament

O Virgin Immaculate,
perfect lover of our Eucharistic God,
you bore the Word Made Flesh;
blessed fruit of thy womb.

Full of Grace,
thou didst conceive,
by the power of the Holy Ghost;
in the fullness of time,
came forth the Eternal Word.

Mother of the Savior,
He lives in the Sacred Host,
you became the God-bearer;
the Theotokos.

Our Lady of the Most Blessed Sacrament,
first adorer of our Eucharistic Lord,
you help us become a living monstrance,
wherein the Lord dwells.

Grant that we imitate thee in worship,
adoration of thy beloved Son,
in the most venerable Sacrament;
the Church's precious treasure,
His Eucharistic Kingdom on Earth.

Mary at Pentecost

As the apostles congregated,
in the Upper Room,
amongst them was the purest vessel;
the Mother of the Bridegroom.

Gathered around her,
the Queen of the royal court,
O glorious Virgin of virgins,
she is the Spouse of the Holy Ghost.

The New Eve,
Mother of the Living,
awaited to bring forth into the world,
the Lord's most precious offspring;
the Holy Catholic Church.

From the heavens,
at the time for Pentecost fulfilled,
the Breath of the Spirit,
descended upon Holy Mary,
with unique fullness.

Our Lady is the channel,
by which all graces flow;
she is the Mediatrix,
the Mother of the Church.

The Assumption

Full of grace,
free from any taint of original sin,
His sovereign generosity radiates,
in a beautiful, perfect harmony.

From the beginning,
chosen by the Lord,
she is the Immaculate Conception,
loving Mother of God.

A heavenly glorification,
of her sacred body,
she passed unto heaven,
from her earthly exile.

Feast ever most solemn,
honoring the Handmaid of the Lord,
her virginal body remained incorrupt,
the Ark of the Covenant preserved.

Her mysterious Assumption,
banished the curse of Eve;
a most perfect grace,
gifted to the Blessed Virgin fulfilled.

Ascending up in triumph,
to her heavenly dwelling,
she entered the royal gate,
above the choir of angels.

The Holy Virgin Mary,
assumed body and soul,
exalted by the Lord,
became more wholly united to her Son.

The Immaculate Virgin,
united to the Source of Life,
participates in the Resurrection;
arisen to her final resting place.

Clothed in splendor,
with the moon beneath her feet,
adorned with a crown of twelve stars,
she is the Mother of the Church.

The Queen assumed into heaven,
reigns as the celestial court rejoices.
Her fiat brought Christ into the world;
lead the way for our salvation.

Holy Catholic Church

Adorned in radiant beauty,
with a shining glow upon her face,
she is a crown of splendor;
the royal diadem,
in the hand of Christ.

Beloved from all eternity,
she is the spotless bride,
making herself ready,
for the wedding of the Lamb.

She is united with the Bridegroom,
the two become one flesh.
The love story between
Creator and Creation is fulfilled,
that which began in Genesis.

Holy and without blemish,
Christ presents His resplendent bride.
In the bosom of the Trinity,
she has eternal life.

Mystically espoused to Him,
she becomes a fruitful mother,
and bares her spiritual children,
as the Sancta Mater Ecclesia.

She is the delight of the Lord,
like a sparkling gem.
Magnificent and glorious,
she is God's most gracious gift.

Acknowledgments

First and foremost I would like to thank, God Our Father, for giving us His only begotten Son, Jesus Christ, my beloved Bridegroom, Who gifts me with the daily strength to pick up my cross and follow Him, and enables me to have the courage to share my Catholic faith and experiences in the form of poetry.

I am thankful to Mary Immaculate; our dear Blessed Mother, who through her own fiat has given me the grace from God to continue to say "Yes" to follow His Holy Will, and to be able to use the gift of writing to spread the Gospel message.

I am grateful for the intercession of God's holy angels and saints for being models of the virtuous life, which has inspired me to know, love, and live our Catholic faith in truth and with conviction, and to be able to complete the publication of this collection of poetry.

I would like to express my gratitude and heartfelt appreciation to my parents, brother, and members of my family for their kind support and encouragement in creating this work.

My thanks and appreciation also goes to all of my friends, especially, the late Joseph C. LaRocca, who had always been supportive and offered continuous encouragement with great love, and prayers for my endeavors.

I hope you have been inspired by

BELONGING
To
CHRIST

It has been a wonderful blessing to write for you.
May you always keep close to the Sacred Heart of Jesus
and beneath the mantle of Our Lady of the Most Blessed
Sacrament. See you in the Eucharist.

Christina M. Sorrentino

ABOUT THE AUTHOR

Christina M. Sorrentino is a teacher in the theology department at a Catholic high school, and is a freelance writer and poet. She is the editor-in-chief of *Ignitum Today*, and regularly contributes to *Radiant Magazine*.

She authored her first book in 2018, and has contributed to various national and international faith-based publications, including *Catholic Insight, Catholic Stand, The Faith Companion,* and *Homiletic & Pastoral Review*. She has also been featured in the *National Catholic Register's* "The Best in Catholic Blogging," and has appeared on Sacred Heart Radio.

Sorrentino is an active member of St. Joseph-St. Thomas, St. John Neumann Parish. She also serves as co-leader for a Maria Goretti Network Chapter, and is the facilitator for a Vianney Cenacle in affiliation with the Foundation of Prayer for Priests. Currently, she resides in Staten Island, New York, and blogs at **https://cmsorr4610.wixsite.com/calledtolove.**

Made in the USA
Las Vegas, NV
24 October 2022

58061800R00049